Water River Run
Ellie Ann Deighton

Copyright © 2025 by Ellie Ann Deighton

All rights reserved.

No part of this publication may be reproduced, distributed, or transmitted in any form or by any means, including photocopying, recording, or other electronic or mechanical methods, without the prior written permission of the publisher, except as permitted by Australian copyright law. For permission requests or bulk orders, contact the author.

The story, all names, characters, and incidents portrayed in this production are fictitious. No identification with actual persons (living or deceased), places, buildings, and products is intended or should be inferred.

Book Cover by Ellie Ann Deighton

1st Edition 2025

Contents

Epigraph	1
Ellie's River	2
Dedication	4
Foreword	7
Water Cloud	13
PART ONE	15
1. Water rushes	17
2. Water drowns	27
3. Water bends.	39
4. Water cleanse.	61
PART TWO	85
5. Sea foam.	87
6. Sea tides.	101
7. Sea life.	115
Water Dreams	137
air breathes light	139

About the author	141
Author's note	143
The Initiates	145
Acknowledgements	147

It is human to feel
~ evidence suggests

FLOW FROM ELLIE'S RIVER

FICTION
Ankhara Codes I: An Adventure to Essence
Ankhara Codes II: Allies of the Soul
Ankhara Codes III: A Devotion To Peace

ORACLE CARDS
Fruits of the Feminine

POETRY
'It' is GOLD
Fire Body Warm
Silver Witch Rose

NON-FICTION
Myths of a Mystic Woman

JOURNAL
Creatively Loving

MUSIC ALBUMS
Temple Calling: An Album For Your Altar

ONLINE TRAININGS & COURSES:
Intuitively Me: The Wheel of Life

more at elliedeighton.com

This is the fourth book of seven in The Elemental Collection; a poetry series focused on the seven essential elements of fulfilment.

You can read The Elemental Collection in any order you choose.

WATER RIVER RUN

To you who flow freely
And to you who have forgotten your flow
We are the same

ELLIE ANN DEIGHTON

Foreword
In my journal I wrote...

August 28 2025

End result: To meet my muse and be informed of the calling of my heart; Water River Run.

I am the magic
And the muse
And I am here
To say to you:

It is time to meet the river
That runs inside your arms
It comes like flowers growing from seeds
Spreading all over your body from your heart
Sometimes you forget
To let the river move
And it restricts you like nothing else.
Sometimes you forget

The river is you
And there's nothing to fix of yourself.
I know it feels like if you cry
You'll maybe never stop
Or if you let the anger open
You'll hurt the people on top
Of the list of who you love
For that's who the river hits first.
You bet, there's a river, in your chest, in your womb
And it'll slam if you've held it in a tomb.
The river is human
It's natural
It's fierce
There is nothing wrong with letting it run
You will feel all your feelings
And they'll move all your stuff
And eventually
You'll remember
We are one.
Eventually
You'll come back
For we are one.
Eventually
It will settle
For we are one.
Eventually

You will see
We are one.
Eventually
You and the river
Will dance as one.
You see,
Like children
They let themselves feel,
They tantrum
And cry
And then it's over!
They don't have to hold it
Stick around in the fear
They feel it
Then did I mention it's over?
This river you will meet
And it won't be the first time
But today
Perhaps you'll let it happen differently.
Perhaps today when you meet it
You'll have curiosity
And then you won't be able to help it,
You'll have to feel
To let it out
To give yourself permission.
To see what's there

To scream and shout
And then, when the river rushes, listen
And afterwards
When you let it all out
And the river isn't dry but it's smooth
You will find a wisdom in the almost silence
You'll find you can come to your truth
And there it is
That freedom
That search we are all on
To really be one with ourselves
To know what we want
To end the confusion
To take the discomfort off the shelf
For finally when the river moves
We can see without fog who we are
For we aren't holding back our sacred expression
We aren't frozen, fearing our scars
We are letting our heart out
Speaking our wounds
Not to hurt but to flush out the past
And when the past moves
The river will clear us
And all we will hear is our heart.
This is the point
These are the moments:
The humanness that can be so tender

That you've been forsaking and it's time to stop,
You can feel and find love,
Forever.
Our soul circle is here for the taking.

Welcome to Water.

ELLIE ANN DEIGHTON

Water Cloud
The Prologue

Once upon a time
The water was a cloud
One day it would rain
One day the sky would be blue
And another day a new cloud would form
And the length of these days were different
Sometimes minutes
Often hours
Even moments
And it was known that the water was merely a cloud
That the rain would fall
And rise again
And the clouds would change
And be back again
And everyone allowed the clouds to simply be that;
Clouds
And all the worries of the world were washed away
Only to return
Only to clear the skies again
– Clouds are made for moving (just like your feelings)

PART ONE
The River

ELLIE ANN DEIGHTON

Water rushes

Under the surface
Even when you can't see it
There is a river
And even when you can't breathe life into it
Because you don't want to feel it
There is a river
And even if you are bored
You are living with a river
And even if you are filled with joy
You will be living with an underground river
And this river
It isn't bad
It isn't good
It simply is
A part of being human
That we all have these rivers
Rivers of emotions
Rivers of feelings
Rivers that are ever-moving
Rivers changing colours
Rivers shifting essence
Like a recipe that can never truly stay the same
Because there's always a different number
Grains of sugar
Grains of salt
You can't count them
And you can't even always taste them
But you know they are there

Oh, they are always there
The world is made of sugar
And salt
And underground rivers
And they can be rivers that set you free
Like the blood in your veins that helps transport the magic of breathing
And they can be deadly
Like the crocodile-filled rivers with a company of hippos
It might seem like peace on the surface
But the rivers have an undercurrent
The rivers are alive
And as long as you're ignoring them
You might not be living
– Rivers are living just like you

I can be in an office
I can live in a cube
I can see only fake lights
I can have only one water on the table
I can function off coffee
I can smile no matter how I feel
I can be in an office
Pretending the rivers aren't real
 – Rivers will make me feel, I don't want to

The faster I move,
The faster I move,
The more things I get done
The happier I feel
But it isn't happy
It's less worry
It's less nagging at the brain
It's less for later
More for now,
Less for later
But the less in the later never comes
There's just more.
More
More
Move faster
Without ever shaking the day off
Until I pick up a beer
Or slap on that music
Or turn on the tv
It doesn't matter really
I've just been moving moving moving
And all I need is to stop
As long as I don't start feeling feeling feeling
At least, as long as the feelings aren't about me
– Rivers are flowing whether we'd like them to or not
– Rivers really are all about us

ELLIE ANN DEIGHTON

You're making me angry
You're making me feel bad
You're ruining me with guilt
You're burdening me with shame
You're confusing me with language
Your behaviour makes me sad
You being late makes me anxious
– Actually, it's my river I'm blaming you for

I'm not numb
I feel fine
'When's the last time you laughed?'
WHAT'S THAT GOT TO DO WITH ANYTHING?!
I yell
Sheepishly laugh
See?
I laughed.
Just now I laughed.
– Rivers aren't invisible, not really

I have a friend

A soft friend

Caresses me

Pulls me in

Lets me soften

I don't even notice

She's hugging me again

And then she just stays with it

Thirty seconds she says

Then our bodies release the happy hormones

That's what she's going for

Both of us having the dose of happy hormones

'You need it nine times a day, let's make sure we do one!'

I roll my eyes on the inside

Always about the happy hormones with this one

I hug

She seems so calm

It's annoying

And then it's the best

I love these hugs

But don't tell her

Even though I think she already knows

She probably does

And she'll keep my secret and keep hugging me anyway

I smile,

It's real this time

She pats my head

No one is watching

It's safe

This is it

It's so nice

Crap

No!

Dammit

No—

– The river bursts

ELLIE ANN DEIGHTON

Water drowns

She didn't have to say anything
She looked me in the eyes
And I knew
I knew she loved me
I knew she accepted me
I knew she held zero judgement for me
I knew compassion
I knew she would be here
I knew she would share life and revelations with me
I knew
And she didn't say a word
− A rolling river helps a rushing one

She's an artist

And a mother

So she probably knows

Mess is okay

Perfection isn't the point

It's only a problem if I make it one

She seems free

Like the kids are teaching her

Play

Run

Laugh

Fall

Get up

Dance

Be wonky

Jump

Again

Again

Again

Learning

Eating

Mess making

Feeling

Crying

Needs met

Happy

Easy

She's a mother

Maybe that's her art
Maybe it isn't different
Maybe it was in her before the children ever were
– Children remind us the river flows

Maybe
If I feel it all
I'll never come back
Maybe that's a good thing
The whole world is different
After a good cry
– Let the water fall

Maybe not
Maybe beavers are an inspiration
Maybe rivers are meant to be dammed
Maybe walls are meant to be built from the bits and pieces surrounding the river
Maybe feeling is a waste
Maybe locking them down is a way of collecting
Of preserving energy
Of saving for the future
A voice in my head
So why do I get so depleted?
Something to worry about later.
Depleted now is better than lost.
Tired is normal.
Can we get a drink now?
Catch a movie?
Have sex and call it making love?
Run it out?
Maybe
Maybe not
– Rivers don't run dry forever

It's under the surface
So I don't realise when I can't breathe
I don't notice when the sky becomes grey
And the grass seems dull
I don't recognise the longing
When my feet haven't touched the grass for months
I don't remember what it was like
To wake up feeling fresh
So I don't notice
That the ache of this tired isn't the normal I have to have
I don't notice
Nobody else is doing life for me or to me
I can't imagine
That this life could be my choice
I can't take self-responsibility
And it makes my relationships harder
But I still can't figure out why
And I'm trying so hard my head hurts
I thought I listened
I thought I did what I was told
But apparently I was meant to read between the lines
Apparently I was meant to notice
But how can I possibly notice for another
When I can barely even notice for myself?
– Numb one, numb all

There isn't less of life
Just less sensitivity
And I can't feel like I'm drowning
It's not that dramatic
It's not that clear
It hasn't overwhelmed me
I'm just... here
And that's all
I'm not excited about it
I don't know why I'm doing it
I sure have obligations
But surely that isn't enough
And yet I act like it is
But I don't know what I'm searching for
I can't know what my purpose is
I suppose it's something I'd have to feel?
– When you ignore the river, you ignore you

Anger tells me yell
Anger makes me dominate
Grief tells me surrender
Grief makes me weak
Shame tells me hide
Shame keeps me a secret
Embarrassment tells me no
Embarrassment is a liar
Anger says hello
Here am I again
Is this it?
– Ignore the river until it consumes you

I'm confused
How did it become this way?
How did we go from living in the forest
Building our house
Sharing our food
Openly making love
Collectively raising children
Sovereignty in our ways
Connectedness on our plates
Waterfalls for showers
Sunshine for morning tea
Tree shade for afternoon naps
Animals as allies
Respect in the mountains
Abundance in the seas
To a box
To living alone
To minding my own business to my own detriment
To paying bills
To lending money
To stressing about clothing
To glorifying education
To broken stories
To silent families
To elderly put away
To pregnancy being a condition
From being a community
To being... well, doing.

To just doing
How did thousands of years culminate in doing instead of being?
How did living well become a luxury for the few?
How did the forest become scary?
It doesn't really matter.
It matters that I'm here.
I'm here!
I'm here...
I just don't know what to do with it.
How do I simply 'be' here?
– Rolling rivers bring clarity if you let them

ELLIE ANN DEIGHTON

Water bends.

So begins the pursuit of clarity

One step forwards

One step left

Apparently I'll know

Whenever I get there

And I'm starting to be open

To dreams coming true

But what I've noticed is that I don't let myself dream

– Even dreaming requires the river

I've heard you say
Creativity heals
But I didn't realise
That even the simplicity
Of writing down my feelings
Of completely making it up
Putting pen to paper
Letting whatever happens happen
Could change my whole world
Could lift the curtains off my eyes
Could bring colour back to the skies
And place my feet back on the grass
I didn't realise
It could be so simple to open up
And so powerful
And feel so light
I didn't realise I didn't have to cry myself to death
I didn't have to reveal myself in front of harsh judgements
The punishments of my childhood don't have to live here
I've heard you say
Creativity heals
And now I've felt it
– Let the river run

I thought it would help
To see the truth
But now I do
And it hurts
I don't want to see
Crappy friendships
And a job that makes me unhappy
And a boss—or wife—who under-appreciates me
Or a child I don't connect with
Or a sex life with no heart
A boyfriend who won't feel
I don't want to see these things
Harsh truths and ugly colours
I just want my purpose
I just want the magic
I just want the answers
The vision of a beautiful life well lived
And all I'm seeing is problems
And I thought it would help
I thought you said this would be the gateway
I thought I was heading for the soul
My soul
Not my pain
– The river changes colour as you swim, but you don't have to drown in the dark blue, you just have to go through it.

The dark blue
Can be depressing
But it can also be calm
Like the yellow can be anxiety all heated up
And can also be happy
I can think I'm about to drown
And take the deepest breath in months
Because I let the river be the river
And then I let the river bend
When I first came to the river
I thought, 'If I should take a drink I'll never make it back
Like the faery realm
Do not consume here!
You shall be caught in an everlasting terror!'
But then I drank
Because it was just a big cup of being human
And the river changed colour over and over again
And I realised this rainbow river ain't so bad
It just is
– All the colours of the river can mean all the things and none of the things

The watering hole
Is a bountiful place
Somehow
Even with all the risk of death
There is all the life I could ask for
There are those who may kill me
And those who may not
And everything in between
The king is here
And everyone else
And occasionally, one of us dies
But we all shake it off
We all see the river flow
We all come back
Because the watering hole may take us to an edge

But it also gives us life
And just like life
When it feels like crying will take you down the cliff sharply
It also gives you sustenance
And then you just are
You're okay
You're relieved
You're somehow more full and more empty
There's less to do
There's a clarity
At the very least,
The clarity says
Go again to the water
– In the water we live and at the waterhole we risk life for the sake of living

ELLIE ANN DEIGHTON

If I were water
I'd be the droplets of dancing rain
Bouncing off bodies
Colliding in joy
Smothered between kisses
One with the spontaneous chaos of life
If I were a river
I would be the one twinkling between toes
Bringing joy through a tickle
And sometimes
Those tickles would turn to tears

Because it would shake off anything
That had been held onto for years
It would be the soul's invitation to call forth
The heart's invitation to let go of the wounds
And the spirit's invitation to flow
I would be the water
And the river
Because I am
And I'm learning that feeling isn't a problem,
Holding it back is
– There's nothing to fear when you are one with the river

One moment
I'm feeling one with the river
And the next
The river bends
And I don't know which way I'm going
And before, when I was one with the river
I didn't care,
I was just flowing,
Happily,
Calmly, more like,
Going along
And nothing else could interrupt that flow
Until it did
And suddenly
The bends felt like interruptions
And anything other than perfection felt wrong
And I felt uncomfortable
I became one with discomfort

And nothing was okay
Everything irritated
Everything made me want to say no
Everything made me want to stop
The river felt wrong
I thought I was getting a handle on it
And then
Bang
Splash
Pop
Just like that
The river bent
I didn't know how to handle it
I snapped and crashed
I cried
I don't want to cry anymore
Why am I here again?
– The river never ends

I'm here again and I don't want to cry
But I'm learning
The sooner I let the sadness be
The sooner I can shift it
– And really, not by doing much, the river bends again

The river was smooth
And I felt smooth too
And then it was bumpy
Terrible
Horrible
As long as I hated the bumps
But when I let the bumps be
The bumps no longer disrupted me
And I could just... be
Not floating, but certainly living
– The river is with us, not against us

The river isn't always meant to be the same
It's meant to twist and turn
And they say that about life
And then we get comfortable
Not wanting anything to change
And then
You can guess
It's inevitable
The change comes
Throwing us into a new river like we're drowning
But I'm not drowning anymore
I've now learnt how to swim
– I started to swim by letting myself go under

I started going under
When I couldn't control the bends
And I began to realise
Magic could be here
At first it was a terror
Only bubbles and white in my view
With the occasional rock and jagged branch tearing at me
But then I realised the bubbles were from my thrashing
This is my river
If I thrash,
The river responds with a force
If I float,
The river calms
It rolls through
And I allow it
And it changes
And I allow it
And it changes again
And it softens
And slowly
But it's getting faster
I can see the light dance through the water
And it's like the very first time I used a snorkel
And I saw magic had been hiding under the sea all along
– The magic is in the river too

Sometimes the river doesn't make sense
I'm upset about Sally and blaming Trent
Trent doesn't know what's going on
Honestly neither do I
And poor Sally, she's confused too
We are all thrashing down the river
Resisting the bends
Trying to hop out when the water turns
But the turns are our invitations to slow down and see.
What is really going on here?
Would be the useful question we could all be asking
Why are you acting like this?
Is the accusatory question we all hide behind
But really
We're all just scared of the river
As if the moment we start floating down
The moment we tip our head under and let go of our breath
Life as we know it will end
The funny thing is
We're acting like that's a bad thing
– However we feel about the river, the changes will come

I have found grace
Under the water
I notice that the surface can be rough
And down there,
Only peace
Only beauty
Only natural order
Even the stingers have their place
Even the sharp rocks get to call this a home
Under the surface
Everything belongs
Everything is okay here
In the way it feels when a mother gently pats your head
Or a sister squeezes your hand
Or a brother wraps his arm around you and pulls you in,
Suddenly
The load is lightened
You aren't alone
Everything is normal
Because it's all going to be okay
This too shall pass
Even if this is the worst
This too will be over
And then we'll be able to pat somebody else's head
And the whole world is lighter just like that
– Underneath it all, rivers run together

I notice when I am around calm rivers,

My own river softens

And when I am around stressed rivers

I stop listening

Because I'm not interested in their advice

Unless I'm considering what not to do

Which can be helpful I suppose

But I find I'm a better person when I focus on the solutions

So I'm attracted to the rivers that flow

Not the ones that have it all sorted out,

Because that's not real,

But the rivers that breathe

They're my people

They're the ones who feel like home

– Those are the rivers who see me

It helps
If a person can see their own river
Because then they can see others' too
And it doesn't become a problem they have to fix
Although some sure act like it
Nope,
It becomes an awareness that can connect
It becomes
I see you
I hear you
I get it
And you have to let yourself change
So suddenly
You don't have to stay the same
You aren't held to the standards of the past
You are simply who you reveal yourself to be now
And there's a freedom in that I've never felt able to explain
– I see my river, I see you

I can let everybody have their river
And I don't have to swim there
I don't even have to visit
But I can lend an oar if they'd love me too
If I'm called to
It's always an option
Never a necessity
Unless you have children, then that's kinda your job right?
At least I'm sure that's what God whispers to me
'Help the rivers that you are called to,
Inspire the rest by being you'
And I've noticed
Sometimes my inspiration comes in the form of disappointment
Of triggering my audience
Because they want me to be the same as my past self
Or the same as someone else out there
But I'll never be the same as someone else,
Even past me,
Because the river bends

Over and over

And every time I notice the bend I learn from it

And every time I learn from it I become one again

And the more I become one the more I change

I forget again

I fall into the pain of being human

And then another bend in the river will wake me up

And I'll change again

So I can never be the same

And neither will you

And life seems like it will be a lot easier

If we let go of fitting each other in boxes

And start noticing,

Allowing the truth,

That we are all floating down our rivers

And we are all doing the best that we can do

– Rivers are universal and never-ending, un-boxable, just like me and you

ELLIE ANN DEIGHTON

Water cleanse.

Sometimes I think
That's not your best
And it certainly wasn't mine
And then I realise in that moment
I had a choice
So did you
And maybe we chose wrong
Or maybe we chose the learning the hard way
But that was our choice to make
And I've noticed it matters a lot less
If I am willing to return to the waters to cleanse
Not to wash it all away and pretend it didn't happen
To wash away the attachment and flood in the learnings
It's spiritual
I feel the funky fluid self float on out
And the flow floating on in
And I think to myself
Yes,
I just needed to dive back in and remember
– You can always come back to the river

The river isn't going anywhere

It's about as curable as your humanness

So, you know,

A lifelong thing

– Might as well accept the river

Maybe you can't get over something
Maybe you notice you're stuck
Maybe the relationship hasn't changed like you said it would
Maybe you didn't try any harder
Maybe the gym membership isn't working
Maybe the food isn't on the table
Maybe you notice you're stuck
Maybe it's time to go down to the river
See what's there
Notice where you've resisted the water flow
Have you built a dam?
Can you tear it down?
Remove the blockage piece by piece?
Can you be honest?
A little vulnerability goes a long way down the river
A little vulnerability opens the waters again
A little vulnerability can be the best cleanse
Be vulnerable for the river
Be vulnerable for you
  – You can move the stuckness down the river too

A smooth damp cloth on your forehead after a long day
It's cool and welcoming and somehow wakes you up
Just like a hot cloth after a game drive in the dusty wilds of Africa
Suddenly you are completely refreshed
– Simply wipe on the waters and come on home

They say everything that happens in the shower
Goes down the drain
So it's a safe space for crying
Cleaning
Wishing
Dreaming
Singing
Or is it you telling yourself that you have to hide?
– Start the river how you have to but don't keep it inside

Fast movement
Isn't a measure of success
When it comes to a river
Lazy floating isn't bad
Crying a particular way isn't a win
Anger in the morning isn't better than anger in the night
It's all just a river
And it's all just yours
And you have to ask yourself if you're letting your river be
Or if you're shutting it off with an imaginary tap
Because yes - it's imaginary!
The river never stops!
But the river is imaginary!
I can hear them yelling
And I have to scream back
Is it?!
Silence
Because they know it's not
– Your river is as real as you imagine it to be

Whether you want to admit it or not
The world is cleaner after the rain
And the world needs clouds
And sometimes the rain pouring down is helpful
And sometimes the downpour is too much
But always
Eventually
It stops
And then the land is fertile
And the green is everywhere
And the abundance flows through the animal kingdom
Everyone is at the waterhole again
Giraffes sharing space with crocodiles
Lions sharing with antelope
Some days there is blood in the river
But every day there is a river, it's a good thing
The river means life
Where there is water, there is life,
While you're alive, you'll have a river
– You can enjoy the water in your life or focus on the blood and mud in it

It doesn't feel like you have a choice
When they come
They
The anger
The grief
The laughter of overflowing joy
The shame
The confusion
The overwhelming liberation
It doesn't feel like you have a choice
And naturally
You don't
So let them be
– Water flows

I want to stop it
When the water flows
I don't mind it for a little bit
It's comfortable at first
Like finally I'm letting the water out
But then it hits this point
I feel ashamed
I want to slow it down
I'm looking outside of me
To see how slow or fast everyone else's water is pouring
And panicking, making mine the same
But mine can never be the same
I can never be the same as yours and my mum's
Or the same as my brothers and his son's
Nope
The more I try to let my water out at the same pace as someone else
The less connected I feel to everyone
Suddenly everything is out of whack
– I've realised the water is best kept at my pace

When my water is my pace
It's an act of self love
To say yes
Cry today
Smile today
Feel today
Be present today
Be alive today
That's a gift
And when I am showering myself in the gifts of my own presence
I can shower others
And oh how I shower them!
I spray so much love on anyone willing to catch it
And even a bunch of love on people I'm sure will never notice
And it doesn't matter
It's all love.
It's like letting the river flow from me
Told my body it was love
And then all that wanted to come out of my body was loving
To me and to others
And suddenly the world isn't so heavy that I can't function
Suddenly someone's slow pace doesn't make them silly
Or make them more peaceful than me
It just makes their flow a different pace
That's it
It doesn't matter
It's none of my business
And I can love them anyway

And if someone's pace is speedy fast and I can't keep up
It doesn't mean anything other than their pace is fast
And it might inspire me
But it might simply make me think
Good on them for being at their pace
And suddenly I can immediately notice everyone suppressing their pace
Some are speeding up and some are slamming breaks
I've been both
I've got a tendency to notice now
And it's oh so helpful
And oh so loving to myself
– Letting my river flow is an act of self love

So what else can love be
If not letting their tears fall?
If not letting their joy radiate?
If not letting their anger release?
If not letting their pleasure flow?
– You don't have to like it all, but you have to love all the waters

It's not enjoyable
Feeling all the feelings
And it doesn't have to be
– Feeling is one of water's gifts

It's a lonely desolate island

Feeling

Sometimes

But it's a lonely island everyone visits

Whether we open our eyes when we're there or not

– Even islands are made so because of the waters

Water

Aqua

Agua

H2O

Whatever you like

Just let it flow

– The water will wash itself away, you don't have to fix it

Whatever
Anyone
Tells is
Everyone's
Reality
– W.A.T.E.R.

Run
Away
Indefinitely
Never
– R.A.I.N.

  Stop
   Telling
  Off
   Rogue
eMotions
– S.T.O.R.M.

Come
Let
Our
Underbelly
Dance
– C.L.O.U.D.

Dry skies
Are okay
For a day
Maybe more
But droughts never helped anyone long term
Nope
Water is so, so important
– Let yourself feel

Running

Running

Running

Is so fun

Until you get blisters

And you can't breathe

And your heart is going to beat out of your chest

And your saliva thickens

And you can't think straight

Or even remember where you're going

Because you need water

– You can't run away from the water you are

Running over dust is different to running over puddles.
Do you remember the joy of jumping into puddles?
The joy didn't stop as a child.
The dust didn't soften with age
It is filled with rocks now as it was then
Which is fine if you have thick feet or shoes that separate you from the earth...
But do you really want to be separate?
I prefer dust on my feet and puddles between my toes.
How about you?
– There's nothing like freshly washed clean sheets and happy, puddle-washed feet getting in them

ELLIE ANN DEIGHTON

PART TWO
The Sea

Sea foam.

All rivers come here
Eventually
Whether above ground or under
All of them come
They don't have a choice
They're all just parts of the bigger picture
All coming together
All part of the journey
All wanting to rejoin
All with a singular destination
All with the same home
– We return to the ocean

Serenity
That's the sense
When the rivers meet the sea
A oneness
A sense of coming back
And realising they were never apart
At once
There's a peace of having returned
And a moment of truth
Remembering
That never were they separate
Never is the water not a part of the sea
Never are you separate from the oceans of our land
From the waters of our earth
For nothing lives without the water
Salty or fresh
They're all connected
Even in the desert
There is a sense of the ocean
Waves of sand
And somewhere, deep underneath,
The rivers
And on the surface,
There are the rivers of all living things
Creatures and plant life alike
All filled with rivers
And always
No matter the how or the when

They will return to the great one body of water we all came from
– All the rivers meet the sea

We might name it different things
Lakes of sadness
Rivers of joy
Seas of sunshine
Oceans of moodiness
Swamps of fun
Call it what you want
It's all water
It's all feelings
It's all free unless you cage it
And really, none of it can be caged
And really, no two people can call it the same
For no two people will ever see it the same
Feel it the same
Experience it the same
– It's not our job to describe the water, it's our job to let it flow

When the rivers start to flow
And you let them
You'll realise you are an ocean
And you will see your depths
You will see your darkness
You will see your bliss
And eventually
On the other side of a process
An awakening of sorts
You will rebound
You will decide you are not the ocean
You will pretend you are simply the foam
The whites on the edges of the waves
Not very deep at all
In fact
Inherently surface level!
Maybe it's because you saw something down there that scared you
Maybe life was beginning to look like it was going to be too good
Maybe old habits got the better of you
Someone put you down and you believed it
You were rejected and you took that rejection to your soul

Maybe
You see realising you are the ocean isn't a one time thing
Neither is feeling the rivers,
Travelling to the sea
You will come to your waters over and over again
And you will realise over and over again
That you are the deep
And you can be the shallow if you choose
But you are the deep
Your soul resides in the depths of the sea
Where mermaids and creatures we are yet to imagine reside
That is where the rivers will take you if you let them
Right down deep to the centre of who you are
And you can come to the ocean,
Feel all your feelings the one time,
Think you've made it,
Pretend you're foam,
But you'll know,
You'll have to be honest with yourself at some point,
That you're so much more than the foam,
You're all of it
– You are the rivers and the waves and the sea

Playfulness resides at the edge of the sea
I saw a video once of a horse playing at the ocean's edge
Where the waves crashed
She played
Free spirits united,
Colliding in a mutual joyous affair
Playing
Alive
Naturally tender and free
And what also resides at the edges
Is a sharpness
Not always
But it can be there
A shell that cuts your toe
A cliff's edge,
Much like the waters of the place of my Scottish ancestors,
Which looks strangely like the waters of the place I grew up in
Australia, with more cliff,

Both are sharp

Both are 'jump in and good luck to you'

There are no safe edges for playing

You can enter where you think you're safe and before you know it you are swept up

Underneath

Can't breathe

Smashing rocks

Can't see

And all you have to do is be honest

When you reach the waters

Is this one for observing or for diving in?

You can be ready and you can wait

There are no right or wrong answers when your end result is divine timing

And you're all of it anyway

– Sink or swim, it's up to you

Maybe if you let the waters lick your feet
Eventually you'll feel safe enough to get in
Or maybe if you dive,
The getting in part will already be done
And then you can simply reap
– Your pace is your choice

It can feel safer in the sea when you aren't alone
Maybe you can't swim
Maybe you're convinced the sharks will get you
So you want to give them another choice
Maybe you're not sure what you'll find
And you can't stand the uncertainty
Maybe the little stingers aren't so bad
But you find it hard to see
Sometimes company is exactly what you need
– The ocean can be a good reminder that you don't need to feel it all alone

There's a reason I have a coach

Even though I am a coach

Even though every day is a ritual

Even though every way I use the tools is so integrated it's automated

I have a coach

Because I can have all the tools in the world

I can experience all of the integration

And I will always be human

There will always be parts of the sea left undiscovered

And sometimes diving in is easier with a cheerleader

– Did I already mention you don't have to do it alone? (We're swimming together!)

I have a coach and I love it

But maybe you have a friend

Maybe a sister

Who will go there with you

If a coach doesn't feel true

You see the thing isn't how you do it

The thing is doing it

Feel the feelings

Write them down

Shake them out

Cry them all

There's no right or wrong

There's just: are you being the sea or not?

– Be the sea

ELLIE ANN DEIGHTON

Sea tides.

I once heard a saying
And I've heard it a million times since
With a bunch of different people credited
So who knows who first said it
Does it matter?
Are we past the point of people really saying things for a first time?
Someone
Somewhere
Sometime
Once said,
'The depth to which you feel your pain is the depth to which you feel your bliss'
And it rings pretty true
The more you feel, the better you are at feeling
And maybe feeling isn't the best measure for success in the world
Because sure,
Your feelings can get stuck
You can be feeling things from a million years ago,
Forget that you're an adult and feel like you're a baby,
Take out an old partner's problems on a new partner's innocence,
Feeling isn't always the best advice

But there is always value in it
There's never a feeling that can't teach you
So in the feeling,
In the broadening of the feeling spectrum,
Lives the invitation to broaden your wisdom
To ask yourself
How old is this feeling?
And maybe that'll teach you where it really came from
Maybe that'll help you see the present situation more clearly
And if you can see more clearly,
Surely life's bound to get better?
Not because life was inherently worse before
Although maybe it was
But because in the clarity you reveal to yourself your truth
And more of your truth is bound to be a beautiful
Powerful
Aligning
Sovereign
Thing
– Your truth is at the bottom of the sea

Gentle

Easy does it with the layer peeling

You can go hard and fast

And you don't need to

You can suffer your way through it by unnecessarily prolonging it

And you don't need to

You can slow yourself down

And you don't need to

You can speed yourself up

And you don't need to

You can feel all your big feelings

And you can still feel like you

– Your pace is the best pace (you always know the best pace for your water to flow)

'I'm not ready!'
I've heard it a millions times
I'd hazard a guess; so have you
And it's not true
Not holistically.
In sales,
They tell us if someone is saying this
There's something they need to know they haven't landed on yet
Something isn't clear
And when it comes to feeling?
Well,
Nothing is clear until you've observed the feeling
Until you've let it move through you
You've validated it
And let yourself rise above
Like the alchemical dream that you are
So if you're thinking about a feeling
And you're telling yourself you're not ready,
Maybe you're not clear
And the clarity is on the other side of the feeling
Maybe you are ready
And this is your ego's last ditch attempt to hold you back
Maybe there's no such thing as ready
And you just have to decide this is your time
– Lean into the sea

I can dare you to lean in
And it doesn't matter,
It wouldn't matter.
I could dare you to do a million things,
But ultimately
Even if you think it's my idea
It's you deciding to do them
So I can yell
I DARE YOU TO FEEL
I DARE YOU TO HAVE A GO
I DARE YOU TO BE VULNERABLE
I DARE YOU TO GO FIRST
I DARE YOU TO LEAN IN
I DARE YOU TO SHOW YOUR CHILDREN
I DARE YOU TO TEACH KINDNESS
I DARE YOU TO ACT LIKE WE ARE ONE
It's always going to be your choice
– Your waters, your choice

When the tides come in
They must go out
And the water doesn't just disappear
It moves
You don't disappear when you feel
You move
The feeling moves
Your energy moves
Your awareness shifts
And this is a powerful thing
Feeling is a powerful thing
Because on the other side of the feeling
You are free
Free to choose
Free to decide whether you are the tide
Coming in
Or you are the tide
Going out
But unless you move the feeling
You'll never be the real you
Can you imagine a sea pretending it doesn't have tides?
Can you imagine the ocean controlling its waves so as not to be too much?
Can you imagine a fish turning off its colour?
Can you imagine a shark apologising for taking a bite?
– Stop pretending you aren't you (you know, full of rivers and deep sea)

It's a bit ridiculous
How separately we see ourselves from the natural world
When we could just close our eyes
Take a deep breath
And remember
We are nature
We are the sea
We are the sands
We are the desert
We are the ocean
We are where the rivers meet the sea
We are the foam
We are the deepest underwater cave undiscovered to humankind
We are all of it
Every stage of the tide
Every phase of the moon
And it's a bit ridiculous
Pretending we are not
– What's the point of pretending we aren't nature?

To be the king
Or queen
Of the animal kingdom
As a human
Is an illusion
Are we truly sovereign if the way we rule the land is by separating from it?
Are we truly the one almighty if the way we lead is by destruction and denial?
It doesn't make sense
If you want to be yourself
To destroy that which you walk upon
To be afraid of the dirt between your toes
To try and keep the outside outside
But decorate the house with plants and pictures of the wild
All whilst wrapping ourselves in polyester and calling it clothing
Don't you remember the sea meaning abundance?
Don't you remember the trees meaning there is water here?
Don't you remember the presence of grass meaning we can thrive here?
Where there is water there is life
And we are water
So why are we forgetting to be alive?
– Are you alive? Because the ocean is.

On
And off
And on
And off
And on
And off
Again
And again
The cycle washes
Over and over
We watch the clothes spin
We hang them
We dirty them
We watch them spin
We hang them
We dirty them
We throw them back in the basket
We're so happy when the basket is empty!
But the basket fills when we are living
So what's the real measure of joy?
Oh,
That's right
We aren't measuring joy
We're measuring to do lists
A different type of success
As if everybody is watching
And all they're looking at is perfection
But nobody is watching

Because everybody is worrying about everybody else watching

So who are we performing for?

An illusory audience within ourselves

Maybe we can hear our grandma saying to clean it up

An old boss told us once and we still hear their voice

That first personal development teacher saying repetitively

How you do anything is how you do everything

Well what if how you did everything was that you lived?

You just lived

What if where there is water there is life

And you are where the water is

And you are the life meant to be living

Not spinning

Living

Dancing

Singing

Laughing

Crying

Not washing

Living

Ebbing and flowing like the tides

The most natural mess and joy that ever existed

– You are the tide, not the machine

Do you ever feel like a machine?
I do
Like I've flicked the button on my settings to boredom
Because I've forgotten colour
And I've decided there must be anxiety because there is much to do
Even though my calendar is spacious
And I've decided that it's more peaceful to be really busy
Because that means I'm important enough to be doing stuff
And of course, I can do more
Of course, I can serve more,
Of course, I can give more,
Of course I forgot to sing today
– Sometimes the tide is out and I don't let it back in

My water has me singing
When I move
It has a song
And when I am still
There is still a hum
And the water
When I let it be
When I let me be
Will sing
Will write songs every day
Will love everyone I meet
Even if I don't particularly like them
Because love isn't about agreeing
Love is about connection
Love is an understanding that we're all doing our best
And yep
Other people's best can baffle us
But are we doing our best?
With what we have at the time, yes
Mistakes aren't black and white
They're all we had in the moment
And yes, we can do better
And we can berate ourselves if we want to
Or we can let the waters move
Understand that was the best we could do
Forgive ourselves
Be willing to see each other beyond the worst things we've done
And sing our songs

And the thing about the water singing through me
Is that it moves all the stagnancy
It helps me see my mistakes
It helps me repair what I've done to my body out of neglect
It helps me receive the beauty in the world
It helps
Because it's moving
Like the tides
And singing might not be how your waters move
But there is a way
Dancing
Laughing
Sex
Playing
Cartwheels
Swimming
Running
Writing
There is a way
Your waters move
Paint them
Move them
Set them free
And you soon will be
– Let the tides be tides

Sea life.

ELLIE ANN DEIGHTON

I went to the cinema in South Africa
One of those wild ones
Where the seats move
And you're being jolted around in the air
Your popcorn flying everywhere
Uncontrollably moving in your seat
I'm too little for this shit
And my feet can barely touch the rests
So I am flying around
Water spraying in my face when the blood splatters
Hectic scenes
I'm in shock
Tits flying into my face
Over and over
The movie was a shit show
But there is this one part
Right back at the start
It's actually a trailer
Where I get to float through the breeze
And dive into the sea
And witness the glory of an underwater oasis
It is peaceful
I am floating
Gentle sprays of water
Seat swaying
Popcorn stays where popcorn belongs
My heart rate drops
My belly softens as my breath slows

I am breathing underwater
Three dimensional glasses
Swaying in the underwater float
Turtles swimming by
A whale
It keeps getting better and better
The more I look
The more I relax
This is the sea life
Sure, things fight and die down here too,
But look at all this blue!
Look at the way the light shines through!
How could anything ever possibly go wrong with such beauty?
– It made me realise how often I miss the beauty here too, right here with my body full of ocean

The sea can feel like a fairytale
Separate
Like everything is beautiful down there
If you leave it alone
It rejuvenates
It sorts itself out
It is a force
And yet there are people in places who destroy her
In an attempt to eat
In an attempt to take from which they don't understand can't be replenished unless they leave it alone
There's a big question:
If we are a part of it, why must we destroy it?
And I think it's the stories that have been destroyed
Like the story of my grandfather riding his horse miles and miles to pick up the butter
And he'd have to wrap it up because this is Australia and if he didn't,
That butter would melt,
Dripping a trail home
Butter becomes water and slips through the cracks
So he'd be intentional with how he travelled
And he'd enjoy the ride
And he'd thank his horse
And he'd bring home the butter
And it was simple
And these stories
We miss them
Between Netflix and nightclubs

We've forgotten the stories under the sun and stars that brought us here
That thousands of ancestors walked the earth for us to be born
And they fought and they lived with the forest and the sea
And now we forget to be with the sea they cherished
Now we forget to feel in the safe time we have which they would have luxuriated in
If only the stories of the land were alive and well
They are
If only we were listening
Some of us are
If only we were louder
Our actions are louder than words
If only we allowed ourselves to be a part of the story of the sea meeting the land and dancing all over her
We are
– We can be the fairytale, we and the sea

You don't have to see
Every single part of you
To know that you are nature
To know that feeling is a part of being human
To know that there is shit in your unconscious ruling the show
To know that you have choice and you can be making different ones
To know that you would be living differently if you were allowing yourself to have everything you've ever wanted
To have it all
You don't have to have it all together
All figured out
All perfect
You just have to live
And focus on living
On moving forward
On letting the sea water move
On letting the temperature change
Being with what actually matters to you
You don't have to personally remove every piece of rubbish from the ocean
But you can decide you're never going to throw a piece in there
You can pick it up when you see it
You can teach children why keeping the ocean clean is an essential idea
You can cherish what you have
You can boldly share your sea song
You can be one with your art
You can raise your awareness of yourself
You can choose the type of person you are being

You can forgive yourself and others for where we are and focus on moving forward
You can do so many things
Without having it all figured out
Because figuring it all out isn't the point
Living is
And the ocean will live with or without us
But oh
How life could be better
If we could simply live with the sea
– Being friends with the world is not a calculation to figure out, it's a flow to allow

We don't judge the sea for having different types of seaweed
Or different types of fish
In fact
We see the multiple expressions of turtles and go
Amazing!
Wonderful!
Beautiful!
Wow!
Incredible!
So why
When we have different ideas
And different skills
And different dreams
And different feelings
Would we make that a bad thing?
The sea dreamt seals and then they were there.
You dream a story and then you tell it.
– Be all the different fish for real, not just for imagination

Imagination
Is a wonderful tool
If you imagine the waters moving in your body
You will feel them
Try it now
Imagine you can feel the rivers
The different emotions
Moving around
Collecting streams as they move
Growing in intensity
Some colliding and competing
Some ruling in the wind
Imagine you can feel the moment
Where all the rivers meet the sea in your heart
And your heart is open wide
Allowing all the feelings to move
It's beyond the blood in your flesh
It's a feeling
An energy
And all the energy is moving
And imagine you're letting it
You're letting your hips move and pulse energy up to your heart
Imagine you relax your jaw and let that stagnant energy flow its way to your heart
Imagine all the energy coming through your heart is cleaned by love
Is lighter
You can crinkle up your toes
And the energy goes to your heart

And now you feel more open
More relaxed
That took less than two minutes
And the jaw is tightening again
Because it's used to being tight
And the hips are still once more
Because they're used to the control
But imagine
Every time you let them move
Every time you unleash the rivers
The sea erupts in you
The foam falls off
And in some ways you might say you're empty of all the stagnancy
Or maybe you're full of the flow
It's up to you
But just imagine you moved every day
All the rivers
Towards the sea
So you could be an ocean
Any ocean you wanted
And you could be free
– And so it is, ocean heart

The deeper the water the colder it gets

The deeper you go the more of you comes home

The cooler the touch the warmer the sun feels when you come back up

– More is a choice of how deep you are willing to swim

I'm not saying

It's shallow if all you want to do is float

I'm simply saying

How do you know you want to float if you've never been underneath?

– You don't know what you don't know, watery one

I'm not saying
Deeper is better and you have to go all the way down there to know yourself or be yourself
I'm simply saying
It's easier to relax if there isn't a monster lurking
– Even sea monsters are just creatures if you look at them

Even sea monsters have hearts

Even sea urchins have purpose

Even seaweed has bounty

Even you are a miracle

– The more you sea yourself, the more magic you'll see you are

Even when you're shaky
Shrivelled
Dried up
Don't want to go there
Can't do it anymore
Have given up
Are all alone
Have nowhere to go
There's a river in you
And you can let it move
And when you do
It'll set you free
Set off a cascade
And it'll feel out of control
Maybe
For a little while
But if you let it flow
Let it move
Let it transform
It will
And so will you
Nothing is the same forever
Not even the sea
The rivers are always changing shape
And so will you
And the erosion isn't bad

When you realise it isn't going anywhere
It's simply moving
It hasn't been deleted
Forgiving your past doesn't mean it didn't happen
It means you can be here now
It means you can have your future
It means whatever you make it mean
When all is stuck
All can move
Even when the lake is glass
You can throw a pebble
– All is takes is a splash

Splashing someone can seem annoying
But eventually they'll laugh
Eventually their joy will open them
Eventually they'll realise they needed the ripple in their river
Eventually they'll be glad they weren't alone and had you there
If you feel called to splash someone
Splash away
– Splash with love and let them do the rest

If there's a message I would want you to take
From these poems
It's to make a splash
To have a dream
And imagine you can go for it
Because you can
And let the rivers run while you do
But be sure to choose your heart, your inner sea
Because anything and everything is possible
And everything is always moving
And you are always connected
– Let yourself splash and dive

Hot water

Will trickle over you

Warm your knees in the bath

Warm your belly on a cold day

Remind you that you are alive

Swiftly pull the ache from your bones

Brew your medicine for you

Burn you if you aren't careful

Help you if you let it

– Every temperature has its place, water baby

When the cold comes
It may be startling
It may be everything you wanted
And more
It may be terror-filled
Chilling you to the bones
It may be moving
Awakening you with eroticism
Or it may melt you
Into a puddle of grief
Until you are so shaken
That you must remember
That the water isn't cold
And neither are you
The water is simply water
The water is what you are made of
And it's only cold because you're telling it, 'No'
– You are supposed to feel

ELLIE ANN DEIGHTON

Water Dreams
The Epilogue

I dream of a portal opening
Inside my body
Through my body
Into the waters around me
As a baby arrives
Water as the portal
Body as the portal
Love as the portal
Grace as the portal
Magic as the portal
Sound moves the portal
All made possible by the waters in my blood and bones
All life possible because of the waters in the womb
Anything possible because a new dreamer is here to dream
I dream of those dreams coming true
For the water baby
Which is all babies
For the water baby inside me
And inside you
– Ever notice when you dream the water conspires to make it happen?

air breathes light
out august 2025

A gentle breeze of AIR

Eyes closed
I can hear it
Winding through trees
Whispering between leaves
Opening my mind
Tickling my fingers
Reminding me
I already know
I am guided
I am meant to be here
I was called to be here
I followed the call
And the answers are finding me
Quickly
Swiftly
Slowly
Presently
In divine timing

ELLIE ANN DEIGHTON

Because I am one with all time and space
And the air meets me with grace
– Air is meeting you too

Air is calling. Will you respond?
Read **Air Breathes Light** from August 2025

About the author

She teaches humans how to live in the light of their true selves and she goes first.

Like an integrity radar

Through life

Hers and yours

She will find the cracks

And spit them out

Until your world tastes like honey together

For she is not here to walk alone

And neither are you.

It is no mistake that you are here reading this.

Is it stories in her books calling you in for a journey?

Is her music singing you home to the temple of you?

Is her curriculum asking you to become more of yourself?

Is now the time?

I believe so.

The scientist in her has a hypothesis,

That you are magic,

The facilitator in her

Can prove it,

The witch in her
Can give you the tools to cast it,
The woman in her
Can celebrate you as you shine,
The artist in her
Is on stage creating beside you.
You are magic,
And here,
You will find that you are home.
– about Ellie, author of **Water River Run**

Author's note

You will never be alone
For you will always have your water
And rivers will always be inside you
Beckoning your return to your ocean heart
You can close your eyes and see the rivers
And you can open your eyes and look for the sea
And you can place your hands on your body and feel the ocean
And you can move your body and hear the water whisper
And even on the darkest days
There can be a light
Because of your willingness to be with your water
And the greatest gift you could ever give yourself
Is to learn to
See
Listen
Feel
Receive
Remember
Play
Speak

Be
Water
And let the rivers run free
– Water is what I teach

And I can teach you to relish your water too
Or you can receive little water drops to your inbox

Subscribe for bonuses at <u>elliedeighton.com/water</u>

The Initiates
The Water Droplet

I don't know when it became so easy to forget
How powerful we are.
I don't know which generation decided
That an external reference was best
And that an internal reference was to be recognised as strange.
I don't know who decided that art wasn't a sustainable career option
and started to spread that rumour
Or that writing wasn't something that anyone could do
And I especially don't know
Why we still agree.
Or maybe I do.
Maybe we still agree because it's what we have been taught.
And maybe the rites of passage in our culture has been lost to
alcoholism and fitting in
Instead of being initiated into being ourselves.
Maybe
We've been so trying to fit in to a culture that doesn't fit on our bodies
and souls
And that's why it feels wrong.
I think of this often,

How fitting in has become a societal priority
Even over us being ourselves.
And I don't believe it.
I don't believe there is anything more vital than us being ourselves.
I don't believe there is any one human who cannot connect and live from the true power of their hearts
And so **The Initiates** exists
To remind you
And initiate you home.
And so it is.

Join Ellie in **The Initiates**, an online self-paced journey into the realm of water and emotional alchemy.

Use the discount code WATERRIVERRUN to begin your journey today.
elliedeighton.com/the-initiates

Acknowledgements

Clare

Mem

Paige

Guy

William

Nicolas

Nike

Cath

Camille

Egan

– Thank you for letting your rivers flow freely, **_Water River Run_** wouldn't exist without you.

www.ingramcontent.com/pod-product-compliance
Lightning Source LLC
Chambersburg PA
CBHW071244070526
44583CB00017B/2326